This book is dedicated in loving memory of my 1st born baby girl, Taylor Amaiya Thurmond 4/25/2007

Taylor, Amaiya, and Ava, Mommy loves you with all my heart! I'm so fortunate and blessed to have 3 beautiful daughters. Taylor, I miss you so much. Words will never express the depth of my love for you. I'll love you forever. I will always speak your name and keep your memory alive. Amaiya, my rainbow baby, your light shines so bright. You've been such a blessing over my life, besides being the beautiful, smart, intellectual young woman, you've become, you are an amazing big sister to Ava. I pray that she follows in your footsteps. Continue to lead the way Baby Girl! Ava, you are the gift that keeps on giving. You've blessed me in so many ways already. You've shown me another level of strength and courage I didn't know I possessed. You have so much character and personality already; its beautiful. I cannot wait to see how you blossom!

With Love

Cherise A. Ackers

I pray reading this book touches your heart the way writing it has blessed mine.

-Amy

Table of Contents

Introduction

"There's no heartbeat". Close your eyes and envision the joy and excitement of bringing your first child into the world. Hang on to every precious moment leading up to your due date. Bask in the beauty that life lives within your womb. Contemplate on baby names with your significant other. Sign-up for weekly or monthly alerts that show the progression of your babies' growth. Find out and reveal the gender of your baby. Set up a baby registry at your favorite baby shop. Celebrate and be showered with gifts by loved ones. Decorate and paint the baby's nursery. Envision taking Lamaze classes with other expecting families. Understand that your new baby will change your life forever and be ready for whichever way it can go, good or bad, get ready. Appreciate each moment because without warning it could all come crashing down. These are things that I wish someone would have told me to prepare myself for; the good and the bad. "There's no heartbeat". These three words changed my life forever. I had no idea just how much those words would impact my life in negative and positive ways. I will hang on these three words for years to come. How could there be no heartbeat? Let me take a step back and briefly introduce who I am and what I am referring to.

At 21-years-old I had been in love with a man a decade older than me since from 18 years old. I was shooting my shot and I scored him. I thought I had hit the jackpot with him. He was desirable and wanted by many, mainly older women, which made me stand out. I was very mature at 18 and it would give the impression that I was much older, not by my physical appearance but by my mentality and how I carried myself. Whenever I stepped into a room, my presence was made known. I demanded attention without saying a word. I hung with a select few of beautiful young women like myself. At 18 I was pursuing a degree in Nursing, working at a high-end department store, appearing to have it going on. We looked great together because it would appear that he had it going on as well. We complimented each other. He brought out some arrogance in me and at the same time, he took away my confidence. I've never been a bad person. I've always had a great heart and boy did he know it. He never had to question my position when it came to him; no one did. I was loyal, trusting, and caring - but naïve. I worshipped the ground he walked on. In my eyes he could do no wrong. He was so handsome with so much swag; intriguing to me in every way. He was my everything. We never argued, and we never got into a fight, until we did. I always thought we had an unquestionable and authentic bond, until we no longer did. He was my protector. At that point in our relationship I felt safe with him. Whenever he was around, I knew I was in good hands. Even when he wasn't around me, I had a sense of cockiness because I knew that people were intimidated by him. He was respected and therefore, I was respected. In fact, even I was intimidated by him, and that made him even more desirable to me. How could someone so perfect, not be so *perfect*? God answered that question for me quickly. This man took me on a journey.

Life is a puzzle, God's puzzle and the way the pieces fall into place is extraordinary. I would've never seen the whole picture of the puzzle if it wasn't broken down into pieces the way it was. One by one my puzzle was being constructed. The first piece of my puzzle happens to be the one thing that I claimed as my biggest loss, not realizing that it was also my gain. I secretly struggled with my faith; more so the faith I had in myself. I didn't have a clue what I wanted to do with the rest of my life and I needed to define what my purpose was. What was I was passionate about? What made me come alive, and what would give me butterflies at the thought of it?

The only thing I knew I was passionate about, besides my kids, was life. I was so afraid of death. The reason I am now able to walk in my purpose is because of my life experiences Who could have guessed that?

I had no idea what I was walking into. I had no idea what was really happening. Oblivious and ignorant to the idea that death could occur within me in the form of my unborn child. No one could ever prepare for what I was walking into.

It's April 24th, 2007 and what should have been my final appointment before my baby was born, well it was just that. At 21 years' old I thought I'd be wrapping up undergrad and getting ready for grad school. I should have been diving into a new career as a young professional. I thought I'd be traveling the world, living my life, care-free and happy. The man I'm with should be getting ready to ask me to marry him so we could start building our family and creating our legacy together. What I had planned is not what God had planned for my life. I never thought that at 21 I'd be planning a funeral; two funerals at that.

One for the living which was me and one for the deceased, my firstborn; my first daughter. I never thought that, the marriage I envisioned would not happen and the child I'd grow to love would not live while in the womb. At 21, I appeared to be alive, but on April 25, 2007, a part of me died, mentally and physically. Things begin to unravel quickly. I found a piece of my puzzle that I never could have thought would exist. This piece was called sorrow. Sorrow is defined as a feeling of deep distress caused by loss, disappointment, or other misfortune suffered by oneself. I've never felt sorrow or pain that wasn't physical. I felt disappointment on so many levels. I was disappointed in myself mostly, wondering how could I allow this to happen? Was I so blinded by this man that I did not trust my own judgement? What was wrong with me? Death never knocked on any doors close to me. How was this happening to me and how would I deal with this? This loss changed my life and my outlook on life forever. I would never be the same. This part of the puzzle gave me something that would stay with me forever. Empathy.

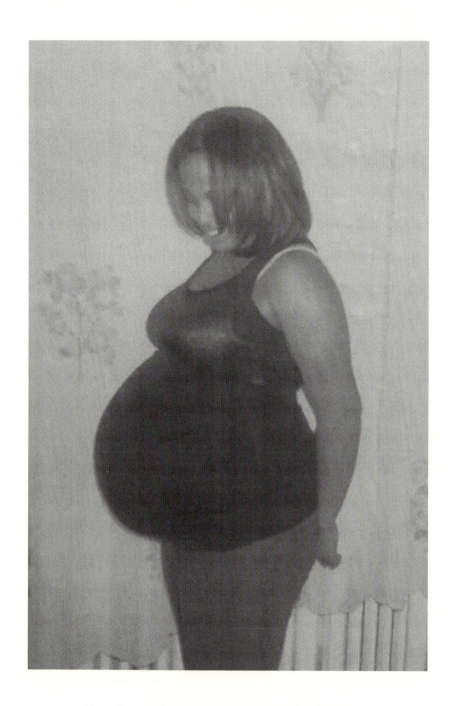

7 and a half months pregnant with Taylor!

Chapter 1

The Hospital

"There's no heartbeat". The doctor can't find her heartbeat. As calm as I appear, I've already died inside. The doctor is just as calm as me as if it's nothing. This doctor has delivered many babies in my family, why would he be so nonchalant and uncaring about mine? I trusted him with my life. I trusted him with her life. I trusted him to do the right thing. What has he done? The thoughts are all over my mind. I have no idea what to do. I followed his lead because he's supposed to ensure a healthy pregnancy, this is his profession. He sent me over to the hospital to have me monitored and reexamined to try and find the heartbeat that he knows is already gone or so faint that this hospital was not equipped to handle. I hear those three words once again, "there's no heartbeat". As I sit in the radiology department next to an outdated ultrasound machine, I'm still unable to process what's happening. I'm unaware and unfamiliar with the process and no one in the hospital was communicating to me clearly what was actually happening. I'm still confused as to why I'm not in labor and delivery instead of being in the Radiology department. Where are the midwives and the labor and delivery doctors? I don't know why it didn't click in my mind instantly that something was not right. I knew in my heart I needed to do something and that I should have left the hospital, but I was scared. Was I sent here intentionally because this hospital was not operating in the labor delivery department? Why was I not being rushed to have a C-section to save my baby? I had so many questions, yet I had no words to muster them. I hadn't let go of my stomach since I left the practice. Was my doctor on his way to the hospital to monitor me? What was going on?

I waited, impatiently, anxiously, and full of stress. As I waited for the nurse to come back into the room, I have already lost my composure. My heart is aching, and I am trembling. I'm freezing cold and shaking. My nerves are shot. I didn't know what to do, what to think, who to call, or who to kill. "Please let my baby be ok" is all I kept saying to myself. I'm holding my stomach, I'm rubbing my belly, comforting my unborn, talking to her. "Baby is going to be ok". I begged and I'm pleaded; replaying every wrongdoing I could have ever done to anyone or anything. I begin recalling memories punishing myself with the thoughts that have surfaced. I never considered my life leading up to now would bring me to this day. I began blaming, accusing, hating, despising, and feeling guilty. I did everything but pray, believe, or have faith. I felt weak and wondered why her dad still hadn't arrived? He couldn't go to the doctors with me that day, my friend had taken me. Has anyone spoken to him? Where was he?

The door opened and the doctor walked in. "I'm sorry but we could not detect a heartbeat. The ultrasound they gave you..." Before the doctor could finish- I blacked out. I could no longer hear or see anything or anybody. I wasn't even sure if I was breathing in that moment. I dropped to the floor holding my stomach talking to my baby. I cried and I screamed, "LORD why is this happening to me? What did I do to deserve this"? I yelled at the doctors, "put my baby on a monitor! Do something! You're not doing anything! What if she is still breathing, and you just can't tell? Get someone in here who knows what they're doing." It was of no use, no one was listening to me. I didn't know any better to leave that hospital and go to another hospital. This was the only hospital I knew, and they had cared for my family for years. My nieces and nephews were all born here- and I trusted them. I was forced to accept my daughters' fate.

She was gone. There was no heartbeat. What else could I do? No one fought for me or my baby. I immediately felt so alone. She was really gone. Yet I could still feel moving around inside me. "She's still moving, check her heartbeat". I repeated these words over and over, yet no one heard me. How could I still feel movement if they were telling me she's gone? There's that little piece of me that knew the fluids inside me were the reason for the movement, still I didn't want to accept what was really happening to me and to her.

Trying to make sense of all of this led me to blame myself immediately. I mean the nurses weren't telling me anything otherwise. No questions are even being asked of me, as if they already knew the outcome. I feel like they all knew something wasn't right, but no one acted on those feelings, no one. Therefore, I thought I did something wrong and that I killed her. I start asking myself questions- "Did I drink too much orange juice?" I was sure it was the acid from the orange juice. "Was it the way I slept the night before?" I knew I must have rolled over and suffocated her. "Should I have not being having sex while I was pregnant?" It was definitely all the pressure from intercourse. "I know, it was because I fell at work two months prior and I missed that one physical therapy session I was supposed to make up". While all the things I was thinking had absolutely nothing to do with her loss, those were the thoughts I was beating myself up about. I was ignorant and uneducated about pregnancy loss.

I listened while conversations were being had as if I wasn't sitting in the room. As if I was not the one that was about to experience this laboring process. I'm still trying to process the fact that I'm just sitting here, and my baby is inside me, but there's no heartbeat. How was that even be possible? Why were those people running around like they had no idea what to do? I vividly remember the emptiness and quietness of the hospital floor. I looked for other patients, but I never saw any. This was the labor and delivery floor but there weren't any babies being born, at least not alive. I didn't hear the sound of newborn baby cries or the screams of women from labor pains. There wasn't any other guest on this floor except for those there with me. I did eventually hear that there was a girl in a room nearby who had been experiencing a miscarriage. Don't you know someone had the audacity to ask me to talk with her because of how well I appeared to be handling my situation? Absolutely not! I may have appeared to be handling it better than most, but it was only because I was just at a loss for words. My emotions and feelings had become numb. I wanted to die. I wanted Taylor to come back, so I could take her place, she did not deserve this, neither of us did. That's my baby's name, Taylor.

Reflecting back, it's so ironic that I was being called to help someone who had been suffering a loss even while I was suffering my loss. That was my calling then. That was God telling me, maybe not now, but I'm coming back to this very calling later on, so you can help others. God was preparing to make me stronger so that eventually I'd be able to be obedient and step up to fulfil my calling.

The phones were ringing off the hook and all the calls were about me. Those people were just as clueless as I was and to add to the agony I already was in, there was a maintenance man in my room doing construction as I lied in the bed preparing to deliver my baby, stillborn. It was extremely hot in there which is what this man was doing, trying to fix the air conditioning. My brother was by my side and extended his hand to help to speed up the process and end the noise the maintenance man was making. It was very uncomfortable and frustrating. What was wrong with this hospital and why didn't it seem like they were prepared to have anyone in their labor and delivery unit? I wondered.

"We're going to need you to push her out". In my mind, I thought, excuse me are you kidding me? How was this day getting worse? How could I push her out? How could I give birth if she's already lifeless? "So, she might still be alive once I push her out?" There goes that little piece of hope that I was holding onto for dear life. At this point I just want my baby out, so I could hold her and hug her back to life. I didn't want to believe I was going to push her out and that she was already gone. Nothing made sense to me during that entire process. The disgust I felt for this hospital was intolerable.

One by one our family and friends began to arrive. I could hear the conversations and whispers, but I couldn't make out clearly what anyone was saying. All I knew was that my daughters' father still wasn't there. No one else would feel what I felt but him. Where was he? I needed him, and he needed me. There's no way I'm pushing her out without him by my side. I knew how he handled things and I knew he'd be in a bad space with the news. Someone needed to go get him and contain him because things could become ugly. This was his second child, his second daughter. I could only imagine what was going through his mind. The last time we spoke I told him I was instructed to go to the hospital because there was no heartbeat, shouldn't he have stopped everything and run to the hospital? You would think that's what he would've done. Had he come straight to the hospital when I was on my way, I honestly think things would have been handled differently. I say this because when he spoke, he demanded respect and attention and it was given to him. No one listened to my little voice. No one heard me. I needed him, but he wasn't there. Once he finally arrived, he didn't come straight in the room to check on me. Why? I remember feeling so bad for him though. How was it that I'm the one laying in the bed waiting to force labor, scared to death, yet, I was still only concerned about how he was feeling. He had no idea the concern and worry that I had for him. I'm sure he had been blaming the doctor and looking for answers from the doctor at that point. I could hear him in the hallway screaming because the door is left cracked open. When he finally came into the room his hand was wrapped as if he just hit something. I hoped he didn't hit someone, he didn't but, he hit the wall in anger. He wouldn't look at me. I didn't understand why he couldn't look at me. I wasn't the only one feeling anger and this is why we needed each other but he didn't see it the way I did, at least he never communicated or showed it. What else was he feeling besides anger? Guilt, maybe? Hmm!

Labor begans and the medicine started to kick in making me contract more and more. The physical and mental pain was unbearable. Still, in a state shock and confusion, at 4:16 am she was finally out. After the delivery I finally broke down. I was in so much pain, still I wanted to hold her. She was beautiful. Her eyes were closed, and she never made a sound. She was at peace. As they tried to repair the deep incisions they made, I laid there lifeless. The sad part is I don't remember what happened next. Did I black out at this point or did I block this part out? I'm still unsure. I often wonder could there have been a faint heartbeat? Could she have had a chance if they would have performed a C-section or even properly monitored her? Almost 10 pounds came out of me vaginally. There's no way that a 9-pound 14-ounce baby should have still be inside of me and to make it worse delivered vaginally. Through all the chattering and conversations, I remember sitting there and my oldest sister holding my hand consoling me, and vividly I hear a womans voice muster, "her body is just a shell, her spirit is in heaven". While this is true, it was not what I wanted to hear. I already knew her spirit was in heaven and she was in a better place, but my state of mind was not ready to have that realism forced on me like that. I held on to those words for a very long time. It's one of the things I held onto without addressing it because it could've potentially ruined a significant relationship in my life. I honestly don't recall ever rectifying that situation or addressing that comment directly, but at some point, I forgave and moved forward.

The next day, visitors were back. I stared blankly with no tears in my eyes at everyone. I didn't know what to say. They're all crying and feeling bad for me and I felt nothing. I didn't feel the third-degree wounds from the incision they made. I didn't feel the agony of having to give my baby to the nurse to be taken to the hospital morgue. She needed to be kept chilled until her body was torn apart for an autopsy. An autopsy was needed to explain why, but I'll never really know *why* this happened.

"God, where were you?" Where was God in all of this? God would never forsake me this way, I started to question God more and more. This was not fair.

Loss

My loss formed voids. I tried to avoid. So paranoid. How do I deal? I can't feel. Unrevealed and Concealed. The pain. Who's to blame? So ashamed. Going insane. God please explain. The grief. No relief. I can't sleep. Disbelief. The hurt. My first. Tears and outburst. Please reverse.

It gets worse.

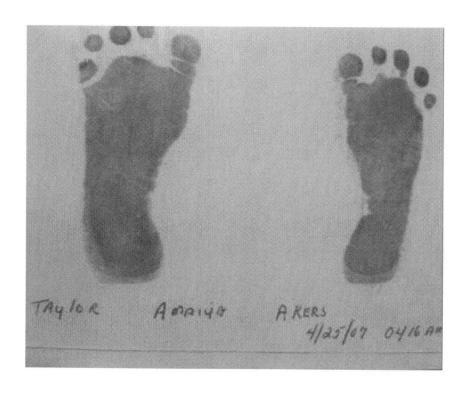

The tiny footprints that left a huge void in my heart for so long.

The tiny footprints that gave me life, after death. The tiny footprint

I'll love forever. The tiny footprints that gave me such a big heart.

Malpractice

You put your trust in the doctors to be qualified physicians

You trust them to make the right decisions

From the state of the patient's conditions

You give obstetricians permission to provide proper care

Ultrasounds and monthly prenatal appointments

With confidences of no disappointments

They say trust us

But when death falsely occurs

Where's the justice?

A suspended license?

That's been renewed twice since!

By Cherese Akers

Chapter 2

Leaving the Hospital

      April has always been known for rain showers and dreary days, but this day was beyond dreary. The day that I dreaded since arriving at the hospital had come. After spending 4 days in the hospital it's time to go home. As much as I wanted to get out of that hospital, I did not want to go home I remember sitting on the bed glancing out of the window while holding back all the tears I had been holding in for the past few days. I didn't want to face this reality that I'd be leaving the hospital without the child I carried for over 40 weeks. As I prepared myself to leave and gathered my things, I felt so many emotions overcoming me. The one I felt more than any at that moment was anger. I was angrier than I was sad in that moment. I could have hurt someone. I was so upset. I literally contemplated my revenge. It's one thing to be leaving the hospital without the baby if your baby was in the NICU or just had to stay at the hospital for a few days, at least you knew you'd be coming back to visit. How do you prepare yourself to leave your baby at the hospital in the autopsy department? If I knew then what I know now

I would never have allowed an autopsy to be performed on my baby. The idea of incisions being made into her body in order to try and determine the cause of her death, devastates me still to this day. If I had been thinking clearly and on my own, that decision would've never been made for me. Ultimately it was up to me whether I wanted an autopsy to be performed on her or not. I wish I would've chosen differently. Being in a vulnerable state is no excuse for any actions I allowed to be taken, but it's an easy state to be persuaded and highly influenced in.

As I was being wheeled down to the car, because the third-degree incision was physically making it unbearable for me to stand up and walk. I remained composed. The halls in this unit of the hospital was empty. There weren't even any paintings or plaques on the walls. The floors didn't appear to have been properly mopped in months and there was no sign of patients. There were no crying babies. No nurses and doctors running around preparing for labors. It was a ghost town in that unit. It still hadn't registered that something uncouth had happened there. No one spoke during the long walk to the car; it was dead silence. It was the longest walk to the elevator that I ever experienced. It felt like this was a funeral. The people we did pass I could feel their stares like a dagger, but I didn't make eye contact with any of them. I feared they knew what just happened and I didn't want to take my anger out on them by cutting them with hateful stares. It wasn't until I reached the door and the car pulled up that I broke down. I wanted to just throw the wheelchair and everything I had in my lap through the glass windows. This was supposed to be one of the happiest days of my life, leaving the hospital with my firstborn and my future husband at my side. My daughter's car seat should have been in my lap with her inside of it, instead I held a purple memory box given to me from the hospital. Inside the memory box has a picture of my deceased baby, her footprints, her hat from the hospital and the outfit I planned to bring her home in. Reality sets in, I was leaving with a bereavement box and not my baby. The life that was planned with this child was left at the hospital. What did I have left to live for? That is when I had my first thoughts that would turn into something deeper than just thoughts. They'd become suicidal thoughts.

I felt my heart becoming extremely heavy as it began beating really fast. My eyes became filled with water. I couldn't catch what little breath I still had. This was anxiety developing, something I've never experienced before that moment. I had my first heart palpitation experience and anxiety attack. We didn't live too far from the hospital, so I knew we'd be approaching home really quick.

As we pull up to the house and I sat there in the car dazing out of the window, I was stuck. The fact that I was about to have to walk through the front door and go inside the house empty-handed had me stuck. Her room was beautifully decorated. Her crib was put together and made up with her handmade quilt and fresh fitted sheet. If you know how good baby laundry detergent smells, then you know how good her room smelled. Her dresser was full of onesies, socks, and outfits neatly folded. Her closet had beautiful dresses hanging, and her tiny shoes are neatly placed on the floor. The very popular, at that time, Classic Winnie The Pooh, decorates the pastel yellow, freshly painted walls. The new carpet smell and fresh paint was still lingering in the air. We were ready for our baby girl to come home, but she wasn't coming home, and I died a little more inside. I stood at the bottom of the first flight of steps and cried for some time. For one, I was scared to step up because my wounds were that painful. I finally made my way to the living room/dining room area and I saw flowers, cards, fruit, and baskets waiting for me.

Cards of condolences read sorry for the loss of your daughter hits me really hard once I was able to read them a few days later. I had really lost my daughter. WOW! My mom and siblings fielded calls and visits for the next several days. I wanted company, but I really didn't want to talk, I just wanted people to be around.

My sisters who were living down South at the time arrived just in the nick of time and I was relieved that they were there. I also felt angry toward them in my time of ignorance because I felt that they weren't here for me while I was pregnant. I had become so used to having them handle all of my concerns and affairs for me that I was clueless without them. That was a terrible way to live in my adult age; total dependence on others that is. Though, in my mind if they were here with me throughout my pregnancy, I would've had more guidance.

While my mom was very present, things are typically received different from your siblings or peers. It wasn't my sister's responsibility, but at the time I couldn't understand that or anything for that matter. I needed to channel the feelings I was having about blaming myself towards others and that wasn't fair. I never told my sisters how I was feeling at the time, I wish I would've, but I thank

God those feelings subsided because I would've hated to ruin the close bond I have with them due to my lack of understanding, healing and grief. All is well.

Totally understanding of how my family thought I would feel coming home to all of her things being visible, they hid things and moved things around, so I wouldn't see it, but I wish they wouldn't have. From the very beginning I hid things, especially my feelings. I think if I was able to wallow in my sorrow more in the beginning, it wouldn't have been so hard for me throughout the process. I didn't know how to grieve because, in essence, it was being done for me, but that doesn't change that eventually I'd be the one who had to suffer from the lack of.

We had been home for maybe twenty minutes and as I finally calmed down from the tears that wouldn't stop flowing, he says he's leaving. "Where are you going, you're leaving me already?" I really only wanted him by my side at that moment. In my eyes, he could make it right and make me feel better. He always made me feel better. Why couldn't he understand that I needed him? What was so important that he had to leave after we just got home from leaving our deceased baby at the hospital? I needed to be held and comforted by him. I needed him to make the pain go away and handle this how he handled everything else for me. We needed each other. Did he even care about me or our baby? I thought a lot of things as he was trying to run off. If I was able to see clearly and if my emotions weren't as involved as they were, I would have caught on to what was happening. What was I missing? It still hadn't clicked that what happened at the hospital wasn't the only foul thing happening to me.

How do I prepare for the next time I see her which will be to view her body before her funeral services?

Broke my water. My daughter. First born. Stillborn. My world. Lord why? The questions. My God. Why me? Why her? This can't be. Take me. The thoughts. The faults. Disbelief. Suicidal, Mind in idle. Throw my bible. I'm numb. How come? This hurts. It gets worse.

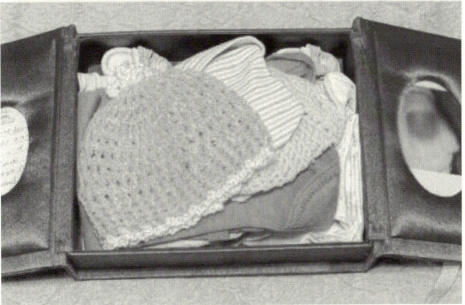

"A Bereavement box would never replace the emptiness I held in my heart, but the gesture to secure her items from the hospital was nice, very sentimental".

Empty Handed

It's time to be released, but I'm alone because my baby is deceased

While at the hospital and preparing to leave

I'm dreading the walk to the car holding my chest because I can't

breathe

There's no baby in a car seat only a box in my hands for the

bereaved

As we pull up to the house where her bedroom is freshly painted,

furnished, and decorated

I carried her for over nine months, and I waited

Every person I see with a baby I hated

Empty handed now I'm stranded in dismay

The visits and the calls start to fade away

By Cherese Akers

Chapter 3

The Funeral

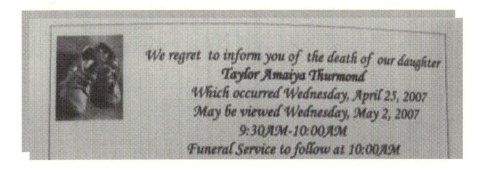

We regret to inform you of the death of our daughter
Taylor Amaiya Thurmond
Which occurred Wednesday, April 25, 2007
May be viewed Wednesday, May 2, 2007
9:30AM-10:00AM
Funeral Service to follow at 10:00AM

The biggest lost I've ever experience was my firstborn. Prior to her lost I don't even recall the last time my family even experienced any sort of loss. Losing Taylor really hit our families hard. We did not know how to mentally prepare for a funeral for a baby, my baby. Thinking back, I understand a lot of what was going on then. If only I were in a better head space, I would've been able to control a lot of things that occurred. I had no control over myself, my thoughts, my actions, and it quietly effected a lot of people and I hate that I allowed some of the things that occurred to go on. Of course, no one wanted to bother me with anything, especially not anything petty but- I wish I had known so I could have addressed it or at least tried to.

My neighbors, friends, family, and co-workers raised money to contribute to the expenses of her funeral. Who would've known that a funeral for a baby would be so expensive? She didn't have life insurance because she never had life. She never took a breath of air, so she never had a social security number. All the expenses for her burial were out of pocket. Fortunately, we were blessed to have a close connection that allowed her funeral arrangements to not require the full expense. The donations of services made it possible to have a beautiful service for Taylor at an affordable price.

The day before the funeral we must view her body. I promise this process was heartbreak after heartbreak. Just when I could stop crying uncontrollably from leaving the hospital empty handed, it's time to pick out an outfit for her to be buried in. When I finally went into her bedroom to pick out her outfit a few had been laid out for me to choose from, but I needed to go into her closet and carefully select her outfit. No one knew I'd been secretly peeking in her room. The first few times were unsuccessful, but I eventually went fully in her room.

When it was time to view her body I prayed that the funeral home did a good job. All I could think about on the way to the funeral home was what if it doesn't look like her? What if they screwed up big time? What if they weren't able to get the red blood off her lips. I would not have been able to handle that.

As we pulled up to the funeral home, I remember seeing my Godfather leaning against his car on the other side of the street. I didn't know he would be there, but I was happy he was. My Godfather was an amazing man of God. Preaching was his life and he loved every bit of it. We had a great connection as he played an instrumental part in my upbringing. He took his role as my siblings and I Godfather very seriously, and I can speak for us all when I say we wholeheartedly appreciate him for that. He loved my siblings and I and he would do anything for us. When he came to visit me at the hospital, I remember him not being able to control his emotions, so he excused himself. Until the day I lost Taylor, I had never seen a tear fall from his eyes nor have I ever even seen him be anything other than happy. He had recently been quietly suffering from early stages of dementia. My Godfather was a brilliant man of God. One of the smartest men I've ever known. He didn't only know about the bible and the Lord; he knew a lot about everything. I wondered why he never told me that there was a possibility that my prays wouldn't work to save my baby. After Taylor's funeral things changed for the worse with his memory. My last vivid memory of him knowing who I was, was at Taylor's funeral. I often wondered if her loss triggered the demise of his memory further because he was devastated by her loss. The last full conversation we had while I was at the hospital, he was speechless, and this never happened with him. All he could do was hug me and pray for me. I miss him dearly. Some time went on without hearing from him. All the numbers we had for him were no longer connected and the home that he'd lived in for years was no longer his home. I know because I went to visit the house and was greeted by an unfamiliar face. We had been searching for his whereabouts for some time with no luck. A former church member from the church we attended as children, where he preached for decades, ran into one of my sisters and mentioned that he'd been in a nursing home for relatively some time. We immediately searched for this nursing home and we went to visit him. Sadly, he did not remember any of us except for my older sister who was pregnant with her youngest son at the time. She looks exactly like my mom and he recognized her. I cried and cried because he was my other father and he did not recognize me, and he would never remember who I was. He passed away years later without my family and I knowing. It wasn't until months after his funeral that we found out via a newspaper article. This hurt us so bad. Still, to this day, I feel so much sadness about him. I never said goodbye to him. One day I will have enough courage to go to his burial site to pay my respects. Outside of losing my daughter, this would be a loss that traumatizes me forever. I silently kept my feelings about his passing to myself. No one knew how affected I was. Being the youngest of my mom's children, I was the baby, everyone's baby, and he was extremely protective of me. He'll always hold a special place in my heart. I miss him. I love him.

We walk in and she looked beautiful. When she was born, her lips were dark red, but they did a great job with making them appear natural. If only I could have seen her eyes, even for a second. The only visualization I have of her is as if she's sleeping. She looked peaceful and beautiful. I pray that she visits me in my dreams one day, so I could see her eyes open and see her smile or maybe even hear her giggle. A minister once told me that when I was mentally and spiritually ready that she would visit me in my dreams.

I guess to this day I'm still not ready because I'm still waiting for my visit.

The autopsy rules that she swallowed meconium which caused her to suffocate. There was no room left inside my womb. She was 10 pounds, of course she suffocated. There's no way that she should have still been inside of my womb at 42 weeks. Or was I 43 weeks? We will never know the truth behind my actual due date. Records had been tampered with, pages were missing, her weight was incorrect, there were so many discrepancies with this loss that it was too much to bear. When we were at the hospital, we took pictures. The outfits that we took pictures in were 3 months and she fit them perfectly. The dress that we picked out of her closet to bury her in was 3-6 months as well.

Taylor's funeral service was really nice. I remember my friend singing His Eyes Is On The Sparrow and it was beautiful. My Aunt shared that she had a stillborn years ago. It was my second, *wow I'm not alone*, moment. Here I had never even heard the word *stillborn*, but she's now the second person in a matter of a week to share this type of news.

If I had known better, I would've had her services at a church instead of a funeral home. Although my pastor was there to officiate, the atmosphere would've been more peaceful in the house of the Lord.

My best friend is pregnant with my 1st godson at this time and I know I got on her nerves so bad. I became really overprotective of her and my unborn god baby. She couldn't tell me something was feeling off or even that she was extra tired than normal without me telling her to go to the hospital or call the doctors. I wanted her to report every single thing because I was scared. I think I scared her. I'm sure the fact that we were pregnant together and Taylor didn't make it scared her enough. I feel so bad for putting all of my anxiety on her. I just wanted to protect her from ever feeling what I felt.

My handsome godson was born just two months later in June of 2007. Whoa, it hit me when I visited them in the hospital. That's my best friend, we're always by each other's side supporting one another for everything and I had to support her on this wonderful occasion. Pregnant and all she was there for me through it all with Taylor. She did not miss a beat and I commend her for that loyalty to me. She sat in Taylor's funeral with her mom (my other mother) by her side. They both saw me through this with open arms and open hearts. She was bringing a new life into the world and this was supposed to be a happy occasion for all of us. I was extremely happy and eager for her, but I was hurting so bad deep down inside. I did not know how I was going to walk into this hospital and hold her hand through labor pains if she needed me. How would I hold my godson for the first time? I had so many thoughts running through my mind, but the one that was most important was for me to show up and be there for my best friend. I broke down in the hallway. I had to excuse myself because I couldn't allow her to see me so emotional because I didn't want to upset her. Her family is my family and they were there to comfort me and so was she. She understood what I was feeling and respected it. Years later our mutual friends told me that when she received the news about Taylor, she was calling around asking for prayers for us both. That's a true friend and to this day we are still best friends and I value our friendship dearly.

While in the funeral procession to the cemetery, someone almost hits the car that Taylor's coffin is in. I can hear the horns honking in front of us and behind us. I saw my brother step out of his car to check to see what was going on. I would not have been able to handle it if her car was hit. It was already way too much to endure that she was gone. When you see a funeral procession, please be respectful and stop. There's a grieving family in those cars and you never know the state they're in.

Funerals are typically known to be raining, gloomy, and cloudy but it was beautiful out. There were pretty leaves on the ground and the trees were blowing from the nice breeze. At this funeral home they have a section of the cemetery designated to babies and children called Baby Land. Looking around I saw cartoon characters on the flat headstones and tiny stuffed animals. My mind was blown away because of the number of babies and children that are buried in this area and it saddened me even more.

As we sat in Baby Land at the cemetery, waiting for my world to end when my baby girl is placed 4 feet under because they do not put babies 6 feet under, I was removed from the gravesite as if I had no say so. I wasn't ready to leave my baby there all alone just yet. There was no harm being done by allowing me to let what just happened resonate. I was in no rush. The damaged had already been done. I was livid. I could barely walk because of the third-degree wounds I had, and I remember clearly being taken by the arm and put into the limo. Why wasn't I being respected? More importantly, why did I allow this to happen? I'm pretty sure that this is the day my resentment toward the people I loved began. The lack of communicating how I felt was becoming the norm for me. Instead of reacting I conjured up this *I don't care* attitude and treated everything as such, I didn't care. It worked for me but not so much for everyone else. I learned early on through this process that people will try to move you. I also learned how to respectfully stand my ground and move at my own pace without being angry with anyone. I reflect now, and it's unfortunate that it had to come to this at that point in my healing. Had I been given the respect I deserved I don't think I would have shut as many people out as I did.

Not everyone will grieve the same way so no one else's process should have been forced on me the way it was. I never learned how to grieve so I didn't. I wasn't allowed to feel what I was feeling without being told otherwise. So, I did just that, I didn't feel. I bottled up and blocked out a lot.

In Loving Memory
of
Taylor Amaiya Thurmond

Sunrise
April 25, 2007

Sunset
April 25, 2007

Service
Wednesday, May 2, 2007 – 10 A.M.
Viewing: 9:30 A.M. – 10:00 A.M.

Julian V. Hawkins Funeral Home, Inc.
5306-14 Haverford Avenue
Philadelphia, PA 19139

Pastor K. Marshall Williams, Officiating

Funeral

Picked out a plot

We found a great spot in what the cemetery calls baby land

God I'm begging you to tell me what's your plan?

We're at a funeral, but who died?

It's silent, No one replies.

Grabbing my chest, my arms, and my legs; Am I alive or did I die?

I let out a deep cry, Was it suicide or homicide?

I look inside the tiny casket and I start to cry

Oh GOD why why why?

I tried and tried to deny who was inside

The feeling I felt is so hard to describe

I'm her mother, I won't let them put her under…..

Take me instead, Take me instead!

By Cherese Akers

Chapter 4

The Confession

I was so blind and so oblivious that it clouded my judgement with everything whenever it involved him. He had always been so overprotective of me, or so I thought. That sense of feeling that he was being overprotective was more so of him having control; he controlled me, and I had no clue. He'd never admit that though. Now that I think about it, I was ok with the idea that his way of loving me was basically secluding me. It had gotten to the point where I was staying in and waiting on him for just about everything. Cutting ties and isolating myself to a certain extent because he didn't like the people I was associated with, family and friends. I didn't know. It's that terrible cliché that always stands true that you're "young and dumb". Well I was young and dumb. He knew my insecurities and the areas I felt I lacked in and believe me, he played on those insecurities as best as he could. I never felt good enough period. I was never pretty enough, or small enough. I was always tall, thick, with big feet and a big head. This is how I felt about myself. So, the idea that this man only wanted me for himself made me feel incredible, confident, and secure. I thought it was cute and here I am, this young girl, and I have this old head who all the ladies wanted at the time. I felt superior and in control. Little did I know that was the last thing I was.

I had just buried my firstborn, my baby girl, my daughter, life can't get any worse for me at this point; so, I thought, silly me. The insults became frequent but indirect. I didn't realize that some comments whether direct or indirect could affect a person so much. The time we were spending became sporadic and quick. The visits seemed more of drop-offs. The calls and conversations were scarce. The affection was forced and bleak. Less and less hugs and kisses. Something was clearly going on. Something or someone was demanding his time and his presence. I heard the rumors but always ignored them. My justification was that people were jealous and hating because of their own situations. We all see the signs for ourselves though. We always know when something isn't right, but we continue to ignore the signs anyway. Don't ignore the signs. Don't ignore your gut instance. How many times will it take before you don't believe the lies anymore? Deep down I already knew there was another woman. What I didn't know was how significant she was, and my rationalization was, how important could she be if she's never around? How close could they be if she never met or been around the family? I was always there, even when he wasn't, so I knew when it mattered, and it was important she was not around. His daughter didn't know who she was, all she knew was me. That was my baby, I always had her with me. Her mom and I never had any issues and genuinely got along and became friendly. I'm the one that's always around. I just had his 2nd child, whom we were still grieving the loss of, and we still needed the comfort from each other. He was being comforted alright, he just didn't want or need it from me. Only he felt what I was feeling and vice versa. And we had also just found out I was pregnant again with his 3rd child. Not to mention his family adored me. They would never allow another woman to supersede me in their lives, or so I thought. These are the rationalizations I told myself over and over. These reasonings made me able to sleep at night when I couldn't get a hold of him. I would tell myself every night that he's working, or his phone must have died, the best one was, he's sleeping. I knew in my heart that he was sleeping, but he wasn't alone, and he wasn't at home because I was. But she didn't matter to me. In my eyes, he could still do no wrong because that feeling that he once adored me still held a big place in my heart and mind. In my blind eyes, we were still a family. Little did I know he was building two of them without consenting with me or with her.

"I have to tell you something". The words that replayed in my mind for a very long time. The words that for the second time in a matter of months almost destroyed me for a second time. The words that never should have been spoken. The words that ruined everything for us. The words that will have a major impact on my sanity at this time. After I stared blankly for a second, trying to process what he could possibly need to tell me, I finally open my mouth. "What's up? You can tell me on the way to my mom's". There had been an awkward silence for a couple of minutes, the music was turned down, and my heart began to race because I knew something was up.

It had only been about three months since Taylor's funeral and I began to feel like myself for a slight second. I'm pregnant. Yes already, and I wasn't sure I was ready for another baby, but at that point I had no choice. No other choices ever crossed my mind. I knew after what I went through that I would never have an abortion or allow any harm to come to any children I have. I was given another opportunity to raise a child and I was going to do my all to protect this child.

"What do you have to tell me? What's wrong?" As he continues to just look at me with so much shame and guilt in his eyes. The look that quickly worried me about what could he have to tell me. I thought first that he was in trouble or maybe he was going to jail or moving to another state. Never expected the next words. "I have a baby on the way; and not our baby you're carrying. She's four months pregnant with my son." I paused. "Wait what, repeat that, what did you say? Say that again." I was not processing what was just said. I needed him to repeat himself. I needed to know that's what I heard. It was exactly what I heard. I could have punched him in his face but immediately I began to cry uncontrollably. I was upset, hurt, and disgusted. I had questions and I needed answers.

Why would this man ever do this to me, to us? We just buried our daughter and I'm pregnant with his baby again. How in the world could GOD punish me this way again? Why was God using this man to beat me down like this? Wasn't losing Taylor enough? Haven't I been persecuted enough? "Let me out this car". I tried to get out of the car because I wanted to hurt him. I needed to get away from him right away. I felt so much rage. A dagger was in my back and in my chest. I needed air to catch my breath. It was disgusting to know that he'd been with me and another woman unprotected at the same time and we were both pregnant. How could he endanger me and my baby like this after everything I just experienced, my body just experienced? I needed him out of my sight for my own sanity and safety.

As I think back, was he even sympathetic to my feelings? Did he really care or realize what I was feeling and how bad he had just hurt me? How I was heartbroken inside? He never really showed any emotion until he was angry. He wasn't even at the doctor's appointment when I was told that there was no heartbeat. But this is the man I thought I was going to spend the rest of my life with. This is the man I thought I was safe with. I loved him. "Who is this woman? Your son?" All I could think about is the fact that I wanted a son while I was pregnant with Taylor. I was also praying this child I was carrying would be a boy as well. I wanted my child to have the same name as the man I thought I was going to spend my future with. My son should be a junior. What was happening here? I would no longer be able to have my junior because rest assured, she was going to give him his father's name. I never envisioned myself having more than one father for my children. I think I realized at this moment that he and I would not be together forever and if I had any children beyond the one I was carrying at the time, he or she would not be by him. My happily ever after was not going to happen after all. I would not be meeting him at the altar. My father was not going to give me away to this man. I felt it in my heart that I would never fully forgive him and be able to move on from this.

Once the truth was revealed, things started to unravel fast. The secrets started to be exposed one after another. At this point, he didn't seem to even care anymore. He never owned up to anything. There was always an excuse and a finger was always pointed, mostly at me. Lie after lie. In my mind she was the problem and holding us back. The things he shared with me about her and her life had me content for the moment that she was not an important factor in his life, she just happened to get pregnant. Young and dumb right? This woman had no idea about the depth of our relationship. She was just as blind as I was. I couldn't really be mad at her and I wasn't mad at her at first. This was all his doings. She didn't even know about

Taylor, so she said. How could you not tell her about our daughter that we just buried or about the baby that I'm currently carrying. His defense would always be that she knew and was trying to be smart and upset me. It wouldn't be long before her an I encountered one another in some capacity whether forced or accidentally.

This was a terrible situation to be in and I wouldn't wish this on anyone. The idea of not knowing the truth because you're lied to over and over. The idea of not knowing if he wants to be with you or her. The idea and the possibility that the family you thought you were building is crumbling right before your eyes was devastating. My second chance with him and our baby wasn't going to happen.

Recklessness

Indiscretion. The questions. Deception. Life lessons. His son, he's not mine. The betrayal, my heart, you win. I can't take this again. I quit, gave up, but we always makeup. Cherese wakeup please don't cover-up what he did, it's not fair. In my mind no one cares. Secluded. Removed. Isolated, I'm bruised. Depressed, feelings suppressed so stressed, unblessed.

Who Do You Call?

Who do you call?

When the one person who feels what you felt is the one person you can't call.

So, who do you call?

When your heart is breaking at the thought of her and the thought of her makes you think of him.

Who do you call?

When you think of him and realize you never grieved her or him.

Who do you call?

When the feelings are too much to bare and your heart is still in despair.

Who do you call?

It's been 10 years but still….

Who do I call when the night falls and the thoughts and the faults and the blame game remains the same?

Who do you call when suicide thoughts get inside the mind?

Therapy declined.

Heart cold as ice, I don't want your advice.

BUT GOD!

When no one even knew.

You helped me PUSH through.

Forever and ever, I will call on you!

By Cherese Akers

Chapter 5
My Rainbow Baby, Amaiya

A rainbow signifies beauty after a storm. Well I was about to receive my rainbow. When you experience pregnancy or infant loss and have a baby following, they're called rainbow babies. Amaiya is my rainbow baby. She symbolizes my hope and my healing.

The hardest thing I ever had to do was bury Taylor. It's a part of me that will never diminish. The pain I feel, I'll feel forever. It won't hurt as much, but it will never fully go away. At the drop of a dime, the tears flow. I feel judged and shamed that I haven't gotten over the loss of Taylor. No one understands because no one close to me has had to bury a child. Why didn't I know what a stillborn was in depth? We talked about pregnancy, childbirth, and birth control in health class in high school, but we weren't told about the pregnancies that end before birth. Or the pregnancies that don't produce healthy babies. Or the wombs that can't produce babies at all. Not all babies are born healthy you know. The conversations about miscarriage, stillbirths, and child loss isn't discussed at home, until it happens, and even then, it's still barely discussed.

The decision to try again was easy for me in the sense that I had just lost a baby and I would not have considered any other options if I were to get pregnant again. A part of me knew Taylor couldn't be replaced but having another baby after not being able to have Taylor, seemed like the best thing to do at the time. I did not necessarily want to have other children and especially not so close after losing Taylor. Mentally, I was not there. I did not want to be alive most days. I just wanted to be with Taylor. Emotionally, I had suffered a lot and my emotions were all over the place. I could not process any of what was going on with me. Physically I was still healing, my body had been through a lot. Those third-degree wounds still had not healed properly and still to this day the scars and the tear is visible. I was more afraid to try again than anything. I thought that God would take this child from me as well.

The idea that I was going to give birth again was terrifying. The thoughts I was having were making me go more insane than I already felt I was. I was terrified to carry a baby again. I was terrified to go through the process again. I did not want to see another labor and delivery room. I asked myself over and over would God take this baby from me too? Was I still paying for something that I had done before this? The reality is that fate is inevitable. Whatever is going to happen to us in our lives is going to happen regardless. Our futures were determined before we were even conceived. I did not know how to think clearly because I still had no faith. I had been blaming God. I never turned to God to help me cope with everything I was dealing with.

My new doctors and nurses were amazing. I was advised early on that I would be categorized as high risk due to having a previous stillborn. Being high risk consisted of several appointments, non-stress test, ultrasounds, and being closely monitored. My emotions were still all over the place and labeling me, high risk, upset me more than anything. This all sounded great, that they'd be keeping a close eye on me, but it was disturbing and terrifying at the same time. I still didn't fully understand, and I took this labeling as if they were saying it was my fault. I had never stopped blaming myself so the label, high risk, was an immediate trigger. I would soon learn that many women are considered high risk regardless of fault. If you've experienced any previous pregnancy or infant loss you would be monitored at a higher capacity, deeming you, high risk. Learning from the women who would be in the waiting room with me each appointment, that they were high risk for other reasons such as their age, or other health conditions, eased my state of mind. I began educating myself on pregnancy and all that comes with it. The more I learned the better I was able to handle this pregnancy. Although I was still terrified, I was confident that proper precautions were being taken.

The doctors examined the autopsy in depth and asked me questions and answered all questions we had. Each appointment was consistent and never rushed. They took their time and made sure I was comfortable. I was unquestionably comfortable and aware of everything that was going on. I would review my charts with them and ask any questions regarding the things that I was unsure about. I appreciated this hospital, the doctors, and the staff so much. Throughout my entire time everyone was accommodating, pleasant, and sensitive to my state and my needs. I had a lot of appointments. Starting my third trimester I was seen weekly for either an ultrasound, non-stress test, or my normal prenatal visit. Needless to say, he didn't miss a beat this time around. He was right there at each appointment, asking questions and making sure I was ok. If he couldn't make any of the appointments, he made sure my mom or one of my sisters could be with me and had him on high alert. He would check in before, during, and after the appointments if he couldn't make them. We weren't in a great space because of his recent confession but nevertheless he loved me and was worried about the well-being of our baby as well as myself.

April 21, 2008, my beautiful seven-pound daughter Amaiya was born. I had to be induced early to prevent the possibility of her not making it due to previous issues. My labor wasn't intense. All the physicians were on point and knew exactly what needed to occur and when it needed to occur. I was given my own large room throughout the five days I was in the hospital. I had to be induced so I had been in the hospital for a day and a half before I had actually given birth to Amaiya. Once the Pitocin kicked in, my cervix dilated to ten, and my water was broken, she was ready. Minutes following my water being broke, I was ready to push. By the time my doctor made it to the room, her head was already making its way out with the nurse's guidance. I couldn't wait, I needed to push. Three pushes and only ten minutes later my beautiful baby was born. Her cry made me cry. There was a heartbeat! Dad cut the cord and rushed to be by her side while I got stitched up. My mom stayed by my side and prayed as I cried. It was a bittersweet happy moment for us all. Only a year prior were we in this same state but without a heartbeat. We all felt relief. The waiting room was packed with family and friends awaiting the news. Joy was heard from my room and my heart was so happy. Leaving the hospital this time was a joyous occasion. When we arrived home, I was content, the pressure was gone, and I did it. I gave thanks to God even though I was still disturbed about the outcome with Taylor. I finally felt something which would help me get my faith back.

As time moved on, he and I still tried to make things work between us even though he didn't just have one new baby, he had two. His son was only eight months when I gave birth to Amaiya. Things were not ok. Things were very difficult. Without getting into too many details, he didn't know where he wanted to be until he thought he was going to lose me. He wanted me to be his wife, but only because a new gentleman was expressing interest in me and he got wind of it. The situation made him realize that he could actually lose me. There were other men out there that just might want me. He didn't really want me though. He just didn't want anyone else to have me. Selfish. Of course, I said no.

It had only been maybe a month or so since he begged me to stay and give him another chance. Although I said no and went on about my business, he hurt me once again. A video surfaced of him proposing to her in front of her entire family, it was recorded and shared on social media. Someone intentionally sent it to me so that I could see it. My first thoughts were "but I just said no last month", what the hell! Clearly, he kept her around and thank God I said no and was ready to move on.

Well that idea of me moving on didn't last long. We tried again, just under certain stipulations. I made him believe that if he walked away from her, I'd give him another chance. My stipulations were that if he called off his engagement and left her alone, I would come back to him. He did just that, and when he did, I made myself available to him again. I made myself believe that I missed him. In reality, I just didn't want her to have him. Petty me to play these games with them, right? Did I want revenge? Of course, I did. But I wasn't going to allow myself to get caught up in his web of lies again.

Once she and I had an encounter, I knew it was time to let things go, neither of us deserved this treatment but we both loved him. I knew I needed to let him go and move on to the best of my ability. Eventually I did just that and I never went back. It took a long time to let go, but once I did, it felt good.

The fighting between he and I became so intense. I expected it because he was still angry with me. In his mind I didn't give us a fair chance for us to be together without any distractions. By this point it was too late because I had finally had enough. At some point, he forced himself to no longer care about me. His way of going about getting over me wasn't nice but everyone deals with their issues differently. He was so nasty to me. Just plain mean for absolutely no reason. We could never just have a civil conversation about our child because our unresolved issues would always come up. He was still the only person who could get under my skin the way he would. We would have arguments that would leave my head throbbing. We could never agree to a solution about anything because who can come up with a civilized resolution through screaming, hollering, cursing and fussing. At times, I felt like talking to him was like talking to a brick wall; it was his way or no way. Most times it ended up being his way because who had the energy to keep doing this back and forth, over and over? Not me.

Moving forward, I eventually grew up and the control he once had over me no longer existed. I had blossomed into a woman and I was coming into my own. The once naïve girl whose mind was weak, and who's actions was to please a man, no longer existed. I had a little girl looking up to me now and I had to get my life together for her sake as well as mine. I couldn't allow her to see the constant arguing and fighting. I had to learn how to ignore and walk away from things I could not control.

Don't get me wrong before all of this we were good. He's the kind of man that would take his shirt of his back for you. He has a great heart. He just wasn't good at being honest at that point in his life. People grow and learn from their mistakes. Regardless of what we go through he and I have two beautiful daughters together and will always have a connection through them. He is still the only person who is connected to Taylor the way that I am and for that he will always have a special place in my heart.

Amaiya

2008. No faith. I'm scared. Unprepared. Round two. Do I dare?

DeJaVu. Feared. Second chances. But who? Amaiya, is due.

Nevaeh. Heaven. I'm saved, it depends. Not yet, some regrets. Not

her, but him. The headaches worsen. Heartbreak. Let me think. You

can't depend. Let him go. It's the end. Begin again. But no, I still

stay. Led astray. Picked up weight. Hair turned gray. No way. Let

me pray. It's time to get away. From the fights, the late nights,

ALRIGHT Lord you're right. Give me some insight.

Save My Sister

It's time that we step up and not step aside.

This epidemic is in our city and its worldwide.

My brothers and sisters how do we provide and guide?

What principles young queens should abide by?

Let her know she can rely.

On us. Let's discuss. Genuine. How you been?

Let out the anger and frustrations within.

Your path to greatness. Is in the making.

Trust the process as you progress.

Be transparent. But not overbearing. Swearing and uncaring.

Set your morals. YES, that's plural.

You have a choice, go out and find your voice.

Live out your dreams. Have some self-esteem.

Show self-respect and learn your etiquettes.

Sit back and self-reflect. No regrets.

Accountability is done individually.

Chivalry. It's not dead. But be prepared.

Persevere. Don't allow no knuckleheads. To interfere.

With your decision making.

Be attractive. Breathtaking.

Elevating by education.

Affirmation at graduation.

Living, not just existing. Persisting.

Good health, good wealth. Less stress. So blessed.

It's time to break that generational taboo.

Let's undo. Society's point of view. It's not true.

We won't be pursued.

Just to be disrespected, confused, or used.

Emotionally, mentally, or physically abused.

PUSH through.

Save my sister.

We miss her.

By Cherese Akers

Chapter 6

Depression & Suicidal

I've always heard shocking and sad stories of suicide. I never could imagine I could become so depressed that it would ever be a thought in my mind. The truth is, ideas had crossed my mind, and more than once. To end the torment of Taylor not being here would have been okay with me. An eternal suppression to stop the depression would have been just fine by me. When the Percocet's were gone that the doctor prescribed to help ease the pain that they caused, and the alcohol bottle was empty, the feelings would slowly reappear.

I began taking Percocet's at the hospital because I was in so much physical pain from the third-degree wounds from delivering a 10-pound baby vaginally. I'm pretty sure an incision that big should have never been made and they knew it. The pills made me feel great, ultimately because I felt nothing, physically or emotionally. They would instantly put me to sleep which allowed me to rest and not think about my current reality. I never imagined that I'd become addicted to them and to the way they made me feel. While the

Percocet's made me feel great, they also made me feel bad. I developed constipation on a regular basis from taking the pills. Percocet's are in the opioid family. Opioid medication can slow down digestion, preventing your stomach from emptying how it naturally should, causing constipation. It had gotten to a point that I would purchase stool softeners and drink Milk of Magnesium, just so I could continue taking the Percocet's.

Now that I think back, no one knew for some time that I was taking these pills so frequently. It wasn't until one day my brother noticed something different about me. I appeared to be in a trance and in a deep daze too often. He and the girl's dad also had a conversation about the pills. All I remember is having the pill bottle removed from my possession and flushed down the toilet. I did not have any refills for them, and I couldn't call the doctor to get more because I had to cease all communication with the doctor and the hospital for legal reasons.

It didn't matter because I soon found something else to compensate for no longer having access to the pills, that equally made me feel good. Was I becoming an addict? Was the pain that unbearable that I would become dependent on something that will ease it?

While, I didn't really like the taste of alcohol and I could not tolerate much of it, a shot or two at night would put me to sleep or just relax me throughout the day. There wasn't a single soul who knew I would partake in a few shots each night just to relax my mind. I definitely knew better. Having seen how alcoholism and drug abuse could ruin lives, I would classify my choice of abuse as being "inconsequential". Isn't that how addictive habits begin though?

In addition to the suppressants I had been using, I was also losing weight. The weight was coming off so quickly that it was very unhealthy. I had never been skinny as an adult, but I had become fairly thin.

In a matter of two months everything ceased when I became pregnant with Amaiya. Those were the longest two months of my life. I often wonder had I not become pregnant with Amaiya in July; would I still be in a bad space? Would I have become an addict? I started therapy in the beginning of my pregnancy. It did not last very long because I felt like it was making me angrier and sadder. If only

I could see that all of that had to come out of me in order to help with my grieving process. I needed to share those feelings early on to help me cope. Instead, I quit and tried to handle it myself. That didn't help one bit.

I was hurting in silence for so long because the confession was too much to bear. I was so weak. I was not strong enough to go on. If only I could see her eyes and hear her cry. Just once if I could hold her again, I would be ok. The truth was, I was not ok. I did so well hiding how I really felt inside that it became a part of my norm and how I lived my life. I was miserable, sad, depressed, and all around unhappy with life. I was completely lost at this point in my life. How I managed to get up day to day for so long was only God. I wanted to talk about Taylor and how I was feeling so bad. I wanted to tell those who loved me just how hard it is to wake up every day. No one barely asked and when someone did ask, I would always just say that I was fine.

I can vividly remember the first time I felt anger. It was back at the hospital while I was waiting for some answers. While all the initial drama was occurring, my friend whom had taken me to the doctors that day, was with me at the hospital and she had her young son with her whom I loved so much. We were practically pregnant around the same time, but her son was older than Taylor, but not even by a year. I instantly felt some disgust and anger toward her because my baby was dying or already dead and she's here loving and kissing on her son. I wanted her to leave but I didn't want to be alone. Why was I having such angry thoughts toward her I thought to myself. I didn't realize at this point that I would fall into a deep depression and intentionally push so many loved ones away, including her. My family and friends still didn't know how to handle me. They were hurting more because I was intentionally pushing them away. I did not want to be bothered with anyone. I was still so angry and so hurt by Taylor's loss and all the events that followed. I was still unable to process the idea that I would never see my baby again while on earth. The man I was with, wasn't with me. The family I dreamed of with he and I and our children would never be. My happily ever after was not very happy.

Little did my family know, at any given day, I could've ended it all. The thoughts were so strong and intense that death did not look so bad. Why couldn't they understand that it was not them and nothing they could say or do would help me? I wish I didn't have dismissed them the way I did but I didn't know any other way to tell them to back off me. I didn't want to be the victim. I stopped coming to family functions and when I did show up, I wasn't very pleasant. I was standoffish and distant. I made myself feel like the black sheep of the family. I don't blame them for not wanting to be around a depressed uncaring person. Only, no one knew I was suffering from depression, not even me.

The only person I really enjoyed in my presence was Amaiya. Amaiya saved my life on several occasions and no one even realized it. She was my light from the very beginning. She was the light at the end of the tunnel I was running through. Just the idea of her being without her mom allowed me to snap out of the deep depression and suicidal thoughts I would occasionally have. The love that I have for my children supersedes everything. She was my reason to live and my reason to keep pushing through. She was my person when I thought I had no one else. I knew my strength when I saw myself smiling through all the pain and hate that I had in me. I knew it wasn't the end for me because I was still fighting, I just didn't realize it at the time.

My family always said I was so overprotective of Amaiya. They often made comments that I'm overprotective because of what happened to Taylor. "Let her be a kid", "she's fine", and "she'll be ok". They had no clue that they were wrong. The more and more I would hear those comments from my family, it made me resent them even more. I always felt so controlled. Everyone wanted to control my feelings and my actions. Amaiya was my shield. She shielded me from myself. In all actuality, Amaiya was my protector. She never allowed me to be sad when she was in my company. She loved on me and would nurture me as if I was her child. She loves me so much. I needed her more than she needed me. So yes, I kept her close to me, intentionally, and I kept her safe, and I spoiled her, and I made sure no harm would ever come her way. I have no regrets, except that if only I could've expressed this to my family and friends at that time it might have helped them understand what I was dealing with a little more.

My depression started early on after Taylor's death. When I lost her, I lost her father a few months later as well. He and I were still together, but we were not a family. What we had went out the door with his confession. I lost a lot of family and friends and more importantly I lost myself. We all know the saying, "hurt people hurt people", well I was hurting, and I wasn't the only person around me hurting. I could not escape the pain. It was inevitable. The pain I had was visible, I wore it on my sleeves. Everyone knew what I had experienced which made me an easy target to put the blame on for strained relationships, and that's fine. I took a lot of losses. I learned a lot about myself and about the people I love. Many words had been spoken that could never be taken back. Many hurtful things have been said to me and out of anger and frustration the only way I knew to defend myself was to either shutdown, exclude myself, or curse everyone out. God spared many lives throughout this process, including mine.

My temper worsened, my patience diminished, and my drive for life diminished. If you weren't benefitting me then you did not matter. That was an extremely wicked place for me. It was never in my character to be so careless, so insensitive, so difficult, so unforgiving. Would I ever recover from this dark place?

Suicide, Pay Attention to The Signs

Suicide, deep inside, the idea had crossed my mind

My pride would always override the thoughts of ending the torment

of her not being here would've been just fine

An eternal suppression to stop the depression as my heartbeat declines

The Percocet's are gone and the bottle is empty, the feelings reappear

Call the ambulance, pause, all clear!

Hurting in silence because the confession that I'm not ok is too much

to bear

The thought of taking my life was too shameful to share

I was weak, and no one knew how much the pain inside of me grew

I wasn't strong enough to push through

I would die just to try to see her eyes and hear her cry

I'd be ok if I could just hold her once more

The truth is I'm not ok, twice I woke up, curled up on the floor

Sore from going to war

This is not what I asked for

At any given day, I could've ended it all

Death didn't look so bad, but God wasn't ready for my call

Put down the knife

God save my life

By Cherese Akers

Chapter 7

Trauma

Every time I thought I was finding a little bit of peace; trauma would always find its way back into my life. Such is life, though right? The devil will attack every chance he gets. Don't let the devil know you're trying to get right because he's coming and if you're not strong enough to withstand the devil's advances against you, he wins. My mom would always tell my siblings and I that the devil knew how much she loved God and that her faith was so strong that the only way to get to her was through us, her children. She would express that we needed to be as equally yoked in our faith as she was in order to prevail in this fight against the devil. I finally understood what she meant by that statement. I realized that every single time I would take positive steps in the right direction to get my faith back and my life in order, something happened that would break the growth in my faith. That was nothing but the devil. While I had a strong foundation of faith praying over me and a praying mother and father, I was not praying much myself.

My life was becoming a constant battlefield. I found myself preparing for war more and more. Getting suited up with my defense mechanisms was becoming my norm. Shield your heart by all means. Don't letting anything get to it. I was ready for whatever, until I wasn't. The love I have for my family is deep. I believe in my heart that the devil knows how to get to me. Use the ones I love most to hurt me and keep me down. That was the goal of the devil.

As I stood at the top of my steps outside of my house with him, the father of my children, I got an urgent and hysterical call that my presence was needed right away. I never flinched. He rushed me there to be of comfort the best way I knew how. I remember the conversation in the car as we were heading there. He was always so great with his words and comfort when it did not involve the two of us. Quickly calming my spirit so I wasn't frantic when I entered the room. I asked myself what I was going to do because I currently was struggling to help myself as it is. I was quickly reminded that I've always been great at helping others than I was at helping myself. I knew I had to do something that didn't involve rage and anger. Rage and anger had become my best friends. They always knew how to handle the situation when I couldn't handle it myself. I relied on them.

As I entered the room, I immediately knew that something really bad was up. I saw heads dropped to the floor and people walking away holding their faces in disbelief. My heart pounded. The drilling of the many questions I had instantly began.

Someone very close to me admitted to having been raped two years prior to this confession. I was at a loss. My heart had just been ripped out again. I was saddened and enraged by the news. Where the hell was I when her innocence was being stripped from her; stolen with no regard to the suffering and anguish she would have to deal with. I thought that what she had already been through traumatically in her short life had was hard and bad enough, but now this?

How did this terrible incident become about me? How did I allow what happened to her taint me this way? I felt guilty and partly to blame. Even though I know I could have never seen this coming, but how could I have helped prevent this? I knew all so well how trauma could negatively impact and rock your world. I never wanted my loved ones to ever have to experience the result that trauma leaves behind.

A million feelings ran through my mind. A million scenes replayed in my head. A million interactions repeated itself over and over. Of course, I reverted back to that dark space. Why was God punishing me through my loved ones? The people that I held dear were being hurt. Is this the attack on my family that my mom had been preaching to us about that I would blatantly ignore? Was I moving in a positive direction and didn't even realize it? Did God want to see how strong I was, or was it the devil showing me how weak I still was?

I secretly was blaming myself. Was I so immersed in my own pity that I missed the signs? It's been plenty times that I've been in the presence of others in the flesh but mentally somewhere else. I stayed in desolation for a very long time. It pisses me off that I was so complacent in my despair. I could have protected her if I wasn't so disengaged mentally. I was good at hiding myself all around. I felt so ashamed and embarrassed at myself. I would never tell this to a single soul though; too much pride.

At the Special Victim's Unit, I sat there lifeless. Again, I reverted back to that dark space that was becoming too familiar for me. This scene was all so familiar to me. Where have I seen this? This was me a few years ago as I sat in the Emergency Room of the hospital waiting to be told again that there was no heartbeat. I'm numb inside but on the outside, I'm appearing to be strong for her. I've mastered the ability to be strong for everyone else, but seldom did I show that same strength for my own needs.

She's so brave for speaking out about this and sharing her truth. I'm very proud of her, but I'm also scared at the same time. How would we help her prepare for whatever comes next especially because we are all uneducated about this sort of trauma? What will she have to endure? I wasn't ready to face all that could possibly come with this, not for my sake, but for her sake. It was necessary and needed to be exposed for her healing process to begin. More than ever she needed all the support she could get. I had to be strong for her while still trying to be strong for my own sanity. Nevertheless, I'm in her corner 100 percent.

I prayed so hard for this situation. I knew that there would be a time that she would need her friends and family to stand by her in a trail. We all had to be prepared and ready for what was about to happen in her life. Trial after trial, hearing after hearing, testimony after testimony, but we had to be there and committed. To sit in a courtroom over and over to finally hear the full testimony sickens me. I avoided hearing her story because I wasn't ready. Fast forward, the perpetrator is found guilty and is serving his time in prison.

Cancer sneaks in like a thief. It picks and chooses who to target, at least that's what we're led to believe it to be. Usually the least expected people are victims of it. Guess what? Here I am again in that dark space. In my mind, I'm back in the same Emergency Room waiting to be told there's no heartbeat. In reality, my family and I are waiting for our loved one to come out of surgery, but we are at the SAME hospital. It was the first time I had stepped back into this hospital since 2007. It was not a good feeling, but I went anyway. Nevertheless, I'm there with my family and we're praying to God that whatever they found could be removed and that the cancer would not take over. Well, here comes colon cancer. Here comes the countless doctor visits and exams. Here comes Radiation and Chemotherapy. Here comes stress and despair. One of the sweetest, most loving and caring persons I know is about to have to experience some hard times physically and possibly emotionally and mentally. I felt so bad, I was angry; of all people, why her? I don't believe anyone other than my mom comprehended or cared to realize how much this situation took a toll on me mentally. I know it sounds so selfish of me to make everything about me, but it was the opposite feeling for me. If I removed myself from all situations, I'd be eliminating the problem. In my observance I was the problem. My energy was negative, it was not kind and I was not someone that could see the positive side of most circumstances. Me being around was not the best thing for anyone in this situation. I never once expressed these things, I just made myself scarce.

Everyone grieves and handle trauma differently. All I knew how to do was shut down and disappear. When I was feeling upset, I would do just that, disappear. I should have made myself more available to help out, but I had no idea how to do that. It wasn't that I didn't want to be bothered, I just did not know how to handle this situation. I could not prepare for the idea that I could lose her. There wasn't an in between for me when it came to life and death. Death just happened suddenly for me and I took that fear and related it to every situation in my life. In my mind, I'm back in 2007 in that

Emergency Room rocking back and forth, crying and pleading, because there is no heartbeat. What I never realized or even considered is that if I never communicated my feelings in all the years I've lived in agony, how could anyone know what I'm going through. Selfish me. I figured if everyone knew they'd just tell me to get over it or question why I haven't gotten over losing Taylor. I never gave anyone a chance to make the decision for themselves, I made it for them.

A few years later and she's still here, happy and healthy. Cancer did not win, and I thank God for that. She plays a significant role in my growth and for that I am forever grateful.

Trauma

The drama with trauma is that it's deeply disturbing and distressing

It's personal and it's depressing

In some cases, it's a part of life's lessons; so, I'm guessing

I'm told the greatest blessings come from the traumatic confessions

Therapy sessions to help lessen and treat the suppression

That seems to consume the brain

Mentally, physically, emotionally the pain from the trauma, it drains

How do you let go, rip off the seal, deal, and heal?

By Cherese Akers

Chapter 8

The Journey of Growth

Trying to be the woman I always knew I could be was hard. Starting over is never easy, but when you do, and you feel great about it, you keep striving. Having worked in retail for 8 years and switching to Academics was extremely difficult trying to get acclimated. Obtaining my degree in Behavioral Health & Human Services was the focus at this time in my life. I believe in my heart that had I never switched from business to BHHS, I would not have overcome my fears in a lot of aspects of my life or my depression.

May 2016 was a great time for me. I've never felt so accomplished. What may be small for most was massive for me. Receiving my Associates degree in Behavioral Health & Humans Services with high honors as well as two certifications was a major step towards my goals. Goals that I thought were buried, but I wore my honors cords, tassels, and stole with integrity as I marched down that aisle. In my mind, I was winning. I had won this battle with myself. I had given up on everything and in a blink of an eye I was earning it back through hard work and perseverance. This was just the beginning for me. The desire to keep going was so strong and I was basking in it. Things were not perfect nonetheless, but for once in my life I felt whole.

Growth

Through. Education. Graduation. Celebration. Elevation. Relaxation on Vacation. Acceptation. No more isolations. Communication. No Confrontations. No aggravation. Lots of Admiration. Affirmation. And Compensation.

Strength

Strength is the state of being strong

Feelings bottled all in and no one knows what's wrong

Mask your pain in other things to try and remain sane

Strength is the state of being strong

When the only option is to smile

Because no one knows about the tribulations and the trials

Strength is the state of being strong

Once in a while someone will ask how are you, I'm fine

Favorite line

But all along

You're weak

Unable to speak

The words that came along

With your grief

Strength comes from the state of being strong

By Cherese Akers

2017 had awaken me in ways I never would have expected. Every year for the New Year my sister would have me write out a list of things I don't want to take into the new year and things I want to do better with in the new year. We would attend church services New Year's Eve and we'd take this note to the altar when it was time for prayer. To be honest I never took this seriously the way I should have. At the moment I took it seriously but after service was over and I went on about my year, I did not put any work into what I was praying for and asking for. I was still struggling with my faith and didn't realize it.

But December 31, 2016, I did not attend NYE's church service. I had a sleepover at my place with a few of my best girlfriends and Amaiya of course. I did however sit down and make my list and I prayed over it and I cried over it. I was real with the words I wrote and spoke. I felt every tear that dropped. I held on to every word I said. I've never felt so close to God since before I pushed God out of my life. I was healing. I was ready. I felt it. The feeling I felt that night alone in my bedroom was divine and so surreal.

While in school I had to complete a few internships. All the businesses I interned with were non-profits. I tell people all the time that I was placed in the internships I had for a reason bigger than you or me. God was still piecing my puzzle together. Two populations that I would have never thought I'd be interested in. Violence prevention and LGBTQ. My eyes were wide open. My heart was so full. I could empathize with each population on so many levels. What I discovered through my internships was that my purpose was to help people. Within these organizations I interned with I met a lot of different people who were dealing with a lot of different things. What I realized is that everything I had been experiencing wasn't uncommon and I was not alone in my journey. Having been so sheltered by my parents and siblings and growing up in Mt. Airy, there was so much I had no idea of and no exposure to. In two short years, I learned a lot. I was open to change, and I wanted it; I needed it. Each population I served revealed to me the need to do more in my community in some capacity.

I needed to add more value to my life and do something more for someone others. I started to volunteer with EmPowerMe. A non-profit mentoring program for young women. I put Amaiya into this program and my niece was also a part of this program. Every chance I get I make sure I tell people how much EmPowerMe helped me to fulfill my purpose and positively impacted my life. If it wasn't for EmPowerMe, I would have never shared my story, started We Heard You, found the love of my life, and had another baby (Ava).

I always wanted a son. Each of my pregnancies were girls. I wanted that bond that mothers have with their sons and daughter with their fathers. I wanted a mama's boy. Little did I know the population I would end up serving would be young men where I would gain 15 sons. In February 2017, We Heard You came about. We Heard You is a non-profit organization based in Philadelphia that provides mentorship to the young men in the community. Our mission is *"To motivate and cultivate young males in our community, by promoting self-confidence, education, respect, value, and employment."* Our focus is geared towards young males ages 11 to 19. We welcome all races and are culturally sensitive; encouraging inclusion in all facets of life. The target age group for our organization was chosen because it's a critical and vulnerable time frame for young people. Trying to fit in, struggling with acceptance, dealing with self-esteem issues, puberty, battling their emotions and mood swings. The need for independence and to express their individuality is very important. Social acceptance, appearances, friendships, and more.

WE believe that it is necessary for our young men to have a safe and nurturing environment where they can learn and build positive relationships. They need a place to be heard and not feel compelled to be someone who always has to be tough and non-emotional. We want to enhance their talents, dreams, and aspirations. We want to help them discover their attributes and teach them how to sustain themselves.

If you have children, or are around children regularly, you know how many times you have said or have heard the phrase, "I heard you." The question is, how often do we actually *HEAR* them? At We Heard You, WE believe that many youth are acting out due to the lack of truly being heard and their silent cries are growing louder. In the society and world that we live in, those cries can no longer be ignored. Our young people are being targeted and negatively enticed in various aspects. We believe that this is especially true for our young male population. We love and truly appreciate all the opportunities for our young women within fellow organizations but feel that the necessary support is lacking for our young men. With so much negativity surrounding our youth from the news, social media, neighborhoods, schools, etc., it is essential that WE advocate for them by being positive influences in their lives. With various programs, workshops, events, fundraisers, motivational forums, scholarship opportunities, initiatives and pure fun - WE can elevate them together!

We Heard You was kicked off in March of 2017 and we hit the ground running and never looked back. I take so much pride in this accomplishment.

What a year will do.

Problem solved! I've evolved. Issues resolved. Uninvolved. Following protocol. Stepped out on faith. I could no longer wait. I pushed through. Who knew? Lord I thank you!

Stepping into my purpose and not looking back! Initially serving was therapy for me. Seeing the happy faces of those I was able to help was an incredible feeling for me. Through this new-found passion I developed is where I discovered my purpose. I have no regrets!

It Takes A Village

In a world where young black boys.

From birth, they wanted to destroy, their joy and their poise.

Used like toys.

Ploys to deploy, to keep them unemployed, unless they'll be the

busboy.

Get back to the back of the bus boy!

They have goals that include degrees and payrolls.

They have dreams not schemes. It seems. They want them to have

low self-esteem.

WE Heard You. WE Heard their screams. We're on their team.

We want to help produce young Kings and Young Queens. By all

means!

Necessary.

Overcoming adversaries. No mortuaries, cemeteries, or obituaries.

No court preliminaries.

They'll be legendary, extraordinary. Never ordinary, their struggle is

only temporary.

No solitary.

Confinement. No police lights and sirens. No FBI indictments.

They're climbing and striving. Grinding and shining. Law abiding.

Citizens.

They're innocent. So significant. So, don't be so anticipant. Of their

imprisonment.

It's no coincidence.

More prisons built than educational institutions.

Where's the solution? Blame the US constitution. For the lack of

contribution when it comes to distribution.

We won't be silenced. We're climbing to the highest. Unbiased and

compliant. Joining alliances.

More effective as a group. Time to take back our youth.

The goal is unity in our community!

By Cherese Akers

Chapter 9

Here Comes Ava

I thought I had everything under control. I thought nothing could be worse than losing a baby, so nothing would ever affect me to that extent ever again. I experienced what happens when you forget that God is in control and you're just the vehicle. 10 years later and I am pregnant again for the third time. It's a girl, go figure. I did not want any more children after Amaiya. I especially did not want any more children after learning all that I learned about pregnancy and infant loss. I was much more aware of what could occur and the toll having another child could take on me mentally and physically.

Understanding that I'd be high risk off the bat bothered me. The feeling of being labeled high risk due to having a stillborn pissed me off. I knew I would be high risk because I was with Amaiya. Mind you, I had a perfectly healthy pregnancy with Taylor. It was not my fault that my care provider did not take into consideration that my child was too big. I had more knowledge about the topic and if I can be transparent with you, it scared me. I feared having another child which made me resort to feeling like I didn't want to try again because of the fear of losing another child. Yes, I had another child after Taylor, but I was uneducated, and I was still chasing a dream that was just a dream. The more I learned the more fear set in. My mind had been made up for 10 years that I would never have any more children. It was personal.

I accepted the fact that I was having another baby although I was not happy yet. It wasn't until about 12 weeks in when the doctors told me I could be threatening a miscarriage, that I had a reality check. It was date night and we were sitting in the movie theatre, I had to use the restroom, but I waited until the movie was over. The movie theatres restroom was horrendous, so we walked down to a department store to use the restroom and that's when I noticed the blood. I panicked, screaming his name but he couldn't hear me. I rushed to him and I'm trembling. "There's blood" I tell him. I see the fear immediately in his eyes, but I also saw so much compassion. His distress wasn't *his* distress, it was mine. He understood what I went through and how it affected me. There're not many people I can say understands what I went through and have never been through it themselves. I wholeheartedly believe he understood, and he felt so much empathy for my emotional state from day one. His concern was for me and how scared I must have been. His calming, reassuring demeanor helps to calm my worries initially.

We called the doctor as we're heading to the hospital. We're praying that there's nothing wrong. He is comforting me and consoling me because by this point, I'm crying uncontrollably again while trying to speak to the doctor. Her words were aggressive, but they were honest. "Two things could be happening, it could be normal spotting, or you could be threatening a miscarriage." She asks me a series of questions. "Are you in any pain? Is it a lot of blood? How do you feel right now?" It quickly set in that, WOW, I really wanted this baby. Would things be different this time around? Was there hope for me after all? God must have put this man in my space on purpose, I thought. Thinking to myself, I have the best partner who genuinely loves me and wants nothing but the best for me and Amaiya. The icing on the cake is that Amaiya had been wanting a sibling for years and selfishly I would tell her to ask her dad to have more children. It was different for her because she wanted a sibling in her house, by me. I never wanted my children to

have different fathers, but it did not work out with Taylor &
Amaiya's father and we tried several times to make it work over a
course of 10 years. I knew I would never go back to him, but Ava
sealed the deal and gave me much needed closure that I honestly
never realized I needed. He no longer had control over me or my
actions. It's crazy to say, but I still felt controlled by him long after
we weren't together. I never allowed myself to trust or fully love
anyone after him. I ruined potential relationships purposely because
of fear of commitment.

Thankfully I hadn't been experiencing any pain and the
amount of blood was not a cause to rush to the hospital. I was given
instructions to watch out for more blood. If within the next 24 hours
I saw more blood, I was advised to be seen in the office first thing
the next morning. If I had any pains throughout the night, I was
advised to go to the emergency room immediately.

I never saw any more blood and never had any pains beside
the on-going morning sickness I was experiencing. FYI! Morning
sickness does not only occur in the morning. With Taylor and
Amaiya, I had no morning sickness, nausea, inability to eat or sleep,
no pressure, nothing. Ava was kicking my butt. Once I was seen in

the office for a follow-up, I made them aware of some pressure I had been experiencing. I was carefully examined, and it was determined that I had a pelvic support problem which was causing the excess pressure I was feeling. What I learned about this pelvic support issue is that I would've never known I had this problem if I didn't get pregnant again. It's explained to me that because I delivered a 10-pound baby vaginally and then turned around and had another baby less than a year later, my pelvic never had a chance to fully allow my muscles to heal. In other words, my muscles were weak, and I'd feel this pressure throughout my pregnancy. I'm placed on pelvic rest immediately.

Despite the ongoing morning sickness, as the pregnancy went on, I became and stayed extremely excited. We began picking out baby names which we selected early on. If a boy, he would be a junior and if a girl she would be Ava. Amaiya and I really wanted a boy, he secretly wanted a daughter. I always wanted a junior. I wanted my mama's boy. A few months later the gender revealed we were having a baby girl. Whomp whomp! It took some time for me to admit that I was having another daughter. I had the ultrasound tech and doctor check two more times to just make sure the gender was correct. Ha ha! Nonetheless, the excitement from all three of us was still very present. My sisters planned the baby shower with a beautiful butterfly, garden theme. I fell in love with butterflies over the years because of the way they evolve. I felt myself to be evolving from a caterpillar to a beautiful butterfly, free and transformed, as I was becoming. All was well, until it wasn't.

It's induction day and I'm anxious, I'm ready to get her out. The last 9 weeks had been exhausting, mentally and physically. My prenatal appointments consisted of monthly ultrasounds to keep a close eye on her weight and the placenta. A few months prior the ultrasound showed a previa which could be dangerous for both myself and the baby if it doesn't move from covering the uterus. Here we go again! What now? The concern was that if it did not move, I would need to have a c-section to avoid any harm coming to myself or my baby. In addition to the monthly ultrasounds I had to have weekly prenatal checkup and non-stress test twice a week. I lived at the doctor's office. It was so stressful and so exhausting, and I was still working fulltime. Ava was heavy, and I was huge. I went out of work a month before I had actually had her. I could no longer take it; it was the bed for me, and I was ok with that.

The wait was over, and the prep begins for labor. I can see the anxiousness in his eyes. He's been quiet all day. I know how excited he is to welcome his first child into the world. I'm praying all goes well. We're all praying and have been praying. Amaiya, her play big sister, and my mom are all with us at the hospital. The four of them never left my side. Amaiya would often peak over at me, especially when the Pitocin started to kick in and the faces and moans started. She was worried. My sweet baby girl, I love her so much. I reassured her over and over that this was normal and that I was ok. Little did I know I was not ok. I felt a gush, I had thought my water broke, but it hadn't, it was blood. Under the sheet that covered me, I sat in a puddle of blood. The nurse who is caring for me at this time is in the room and as she's checking me out, I don't hear Ava's heartbeat on the monitor anymore. "You need to get the doctor in here right now because I'm bleeding, and I don't hear her heartbeat". Can you imagine where I went when this happened? That's right, I was back in that room from 11 years ago when those words first were said, "there's no heartbeat". My family rushed out to look for help and more nurses and doctors rushed in to see what was happening. I'm panicking once again, he has my hand, and they have Amaiya. "Where is this blood coming from and why can't you find her heartbeat?" She keeps trying and eventually once I laid back and calm down some, she finds her heartbeat. Ava is back on the monitor and looking good, but we were still unclear about the blood. The bleeding stops and there was some rupturing, but everything appeared to be fine. These doctors and nurses were all over it and I felt safe. I was finally able to rest and got some much-needed sleep.

After being in the hospital for 15 hours trying to thin out my cervix and induce labor, my cervix was finally dilated, and my water was broken. Just a few short minutes after my water was broke, I felt the need to push. It was time. Ava had finally shifted and was ready to come out. Thank you God! My legs were dead from the epidural medicine which was making it really hard to push. I had to hold my legs and put my chin in my chest in order to push. I was using all my upper body strength and I would pay for it later. After maybe 10 pushes and 8 pounds 9 ounces later, Ava was out. She was given to me for skin to skin contact right away. I was overjoyed, but something was wrong with me. As I'm being stitched, I feel lightheaded and I was cold. I felt another big gush of blood come out. The doctor has to press on my stomach to make sure everything is out especially all of the placenta. We learn that part of the placenta had torn which caused the initial gush of blood. They have to remove the baby from my chest because I am crying uncontrollably because of the pain from the doctor doing what needs to be done to stop the blood. My pressure and my oxygen were dropping lower and lower which explains why I was feeling lightheaded and sleepy. A medication is administered into the IV which brings my pressure back up and I'm given oxygen until everything is elevated. I have never in my life felt this way. I thought I was going to die while both of my children were sitting in the same room. As all of this is happening, a memory surfaced from when I was in labor with Taylor that I had blocked out. I was crying to Taylor while having Ava and with all of the people in the room, no one heard the real pain through those tears and the repeated, I'm sorry, I kept saying. I kept telling Taylor I was sorry in this memory that came back to me. It was so intense and so scary. Something hit me hard emotionally because I was so sad after I had Ava when I should have been happy. This was a special time for my family, and I couldn't even look at my baby. I didn't know what was wrong with me. I cried out to two nurses who were trying to force me to move from labor and delivery to the other side. "I'm not ready." Physically I was in pain. My upper body strength was gone, leaving me paralyzed it felt. It was so painful that I could not hold Ava by myself for a few days. Trying to nurse her was extremely hard because it required me to hold and adjust her head so that she would latch on. The only way my muscles begin to relax was through massages with Bengay.

Once we were home and settled in is when the anxiety really kicked in. Everything was 100 percent more intense than it needed to be. I was apologetic and emotional about everything. I didn't have an appetite which was a problem because I was still required to take medication. I worried about everything. I was worried about missing Amaiya's first day of school and risking her feeling like I wasn't there for her. She never said that to me, but I couldn't help but to think that's what she was thinking. I felt like a terrible mother not being able to be there for her. My family all jumped in and helped out where they could. It's nice to have a great support system when you're in need.

I didn't want to be left alone, especially with the baby. I didn't know how I was going to take care of this baby because I couldn't even function myself. What in the world was going on? We were all confused until it hit me that I was experiencing postpartum depression. It was briefly discussed with me in the hospital, but I don't think I knew I was in a funk until I got home. I began to cry about every little thing. Everything was fault, in my mind and I couldn't stop apologizing to everyone.

Six weeks later while at my postpartum checkup I'm given a survey which allows the doctor to see if I am doing well within my physical state as well as my emotional state. The results are in and they disclose that I was suffering from Postpartum Depression. I could not believe that there was another layer of pain and mental agony that could impact me how I was impacted by losing Taylor. What the hell was this and why was I being tested again? Of course, two things are initially recommended; the first being medication, Zoloft, and the other is therapy. I denied the Zoloft right off the back because I already know that I could become addicted to how it would make me feel. I never used another drug after I became dependent on Percocet's. I took the therapy recommendation. She was great. I had the luxury of being able to speak to her via conference calls which was much more convenient as I was not comfortable driving with the baby in the car yet; another one of my many anxieties.

Realizing that I needed to get out the house, I started to drive more and make store runs just to get some fresh air. I also went back to work earlier than I had planned. I started to devote my energy into reading more and talking to God. It was working for some time until I began to spiral back into the same state.

Being away from my infant for so many hours of the day became extremely overwhelming and sad for me. I was at work and away from my kids more than I was home with them. I had already missed out on much needed bonding time with Ava early on, that being away was taking a toll on me. Not to mention the stress that I was having on the job making it that much worse to cope. The goal was to get out the house and get back into the swing of things to help with the postpartum, not further stress me. The decision to cut my work hours in half was the best thing I could've done for my mental health and for my family. I made the ultimate sacrifice and I have no regrets about it. I'm in a good space. I'm able to take Amaiya to school and pick her up as well. The excitement of seeing your child run to the car to greet you and her baby sister makes it all worth it.

Things aren't perfect, but they're working. I stayed obedient and I trust God will continue to see me through.

The blessing in all of this is that I learned from another life experience. One thing, I am is a survivor and I'm a fighter. I never fully gave up on myself. I knew that this too would be a part of my testimony and would pass. I now have another layer to add to my story that would also benefit others. Because just like pregnancy and infant loss, postpartum is not a subject that is discussed until you have a baby and actually experience it. I'll live another day to tell my story.

I'm fortunate to have the support system I have. It is a blessing!

As I reflect on everything I've been through and how I've been

blessed to still come out on top by overcoming so many obstacles

thrown my way. Life isn't perfect, but the peace of mind I've

been blessed with, is everything!

Chapter 10 – I am 1 in 4

Not every child is born healthy or even alive. Did you know that 1 in 4 women will experience pregnancy or infant loss? I didn't know. I've learned that the conversation about pregnancy and infant loss is not common and simply taboo because of the sensitive nature of the subject. The ignorance comes from the lack of discussion. From my experience, pregnancy and infant loss is one of the roughest topics to discuss or engage in. Losing a child in any capacity is upsetting and unthinkable, but it happens during pregnancy and infant stages more often than we realize. There is a numerous number of women and men around the world suffering and grieving in silence. Why do we grieve in silence? From my personal experience it's because of the shame. Many people have no idea what to say which leaves you to not talk about it and just bottle up those feelings. I was always afraid of what may be said to me in response. I was a ticking time bomb and could not handle any ignorant exchanges about my loss. It took me 10 years to speak out about losing Taylor. For 10 years I fought a deep battle inside of my mind, by myself. I will never be silent again.

Speaking My Child's Name is Comfort

Be a listening ear. I don't recommend saying too much unless asked. But the worst thing you can do is act as if my baby didn't exist. Don't be afraid to mention my child. Speak her name. The idea that you'll offend or hurt the grieving parent is completely misconstrued. The damage is already done. You're not making me sad by mentioning Taylor, you're making me sad by ignoring the fact that she existed. Remember my baby with me, it's very comforting. The reason why I grieved in silence is because everyone around me was clearly afraid to mention my baby. I altered how I grieved by not grieving at all which turned into anger and resentment toward everyone. Allow your loved ones to grieve at their own pace and how they need to. Comfort them by reassuring your support. While you may never understand wholly what he or she may be experiencing it is extremely important that you acknowledge that he/she is grieving. Offer support by just being there for her/him. If you're able to attend support and grief groups, I highly recommend it. There's nothing more comforting to know that you have a support system that is willing to hold your hand through this process.

Support the Father

Never forget that fathers grieve too. Fathers may not carry the physical pain that a mother does from losing a child, but they carry the mental and emotional pain. We often forget about the fathers because they're typically concerned about the well-being of the mother and making sure she is ok. Often, fathers appear to have it altogether. Don't let the outward appearance fool you from the inward feelings. Ask dad how he is and if he needs anything as well. Sometimes dad doesn't share how he feels about his loss, but from experience, dad wants to be heard as well.

Early on in life, men are taught that they need to be strong, tough, and confident. Not wanting to appear emasculated, men equate emotions with weakness and can become what's preconceived as non-emotional. In fact, I know that men do suffer emotionally due to the loss of a child just as much as a mother does.

The first time I saw my dad cry was at Taylor's funeral. The first and last time I saw Taylor's father cry was when we lost her. Do not disregard the feelings of a man. Please, I beg of you.

Some things NOT to say (from my personal experience)

- You can just try again. (As if the child that passed away wasn't significant enough.)

- Knowing that someone has previously lost a baby and becomes pregnant again and you tell her/him "now you'll have a child or be a mother/father" (News flash, the baby that they lost still made her/him a parent.)

- My personal biggest pet peeve is "you know that everything happens for a reason" What's the reason? I'll never know. So, for me, death is inevitable, and fate is fate no matter when it occurs.

- "Maybe it's for the best" How is losing the child I loved and wanted for the best under any circumstance? (Always ask yourself this before ever saying those words to a grieving parent).

- How did she/he die? Always make sure the person whom you are asking this sensitive question has the mental space to answer this. Do not assume someone is ready to discuss their loss. Be patient. Be kind.

- This is unrelated to pregnancy and infant loss, but I feel I need to share this. NEVER ask a woman without children what are they waiting for? Or are you trying? Or anything that could be remotely offensive. You never know what she's experiencing surrounding getting pregnant. Not every womb is naturally equipped to bear children. Some women have to have procedures done in order to get their womb ready and in some cases, it's just not possible. Let's me more mindful when we ask certain questions.

Do the Research

Do not assume that a stillbirth and a miscarriage is the same thing. A miscarriage ends before 24 weeks and a stillbirth ends after 24 weeks. I can remember countless times that people who lack the knowledge surrounding this sensitive subject have unintentionally made comments to me that were very hurtful and offensive. While I used to get very upset and react aggressively a part of me knew that it wasn't intentional. I was hurting and unaware of the lack of information circulating about pregnancy and infant loss. Most people who were sensitive have either experienced a loss or know of someone who has, therefore making them relatable. The number of persons aware was way less than the number or persons unaware. The idea that conversations surrounding something that occurs so often aren't being had is mind blowing. Not all pregnancies are normal. Not all babies are born healthy. These are facts that people don't want to face, but it is true. We must start educating our young not just about the birds and the bees but also about procreation. Why aren't our doctors having these conversations before the traumatic experience occurs? We discuss life & death changing consequences with our doctors such as diabetes, cancer, HIV/Aids, etc. Childbearing is also a life changing occurrence. We should not just hear about childbearing once we are pregnant, it's too late at that point.

Speak with confidence because you have researched this topic in some capacity. Knowing and understanding statistics and facts make you 100% more supportive to your loved one. It makes me feel so good when I'm having a conversation around pregnancy and infant loss and someone tells me something, they learned that I did not know.

Note to grieving families from the Author

You're grieving a significant loss. You are normal. You are not broken. You will make it through. You are resilient. You are strong. You are brave. The easiest way to avoid getting upset with family and friends is to simply tell the truth about how you feel. Demand your respect, respectfully of course, to those who have no regard for your child that isn't physically here. The truth of the matter is that until you experience losing your child, you will never fully understand how it feels. So, don't punish your loved ones for trying to understand, educate them on how you're feeling. Always speak your truth.

Speak their names and never feel bad about it. Hearing someone reference my Taylor by her name makes my heart smile. It's an amazing feeling. Celebrate your child as if he/she was still here. There's nothing wrong with acknowledging that this is year 12 and I want to do a balloon release in remembrance of my child.

I can recall on multiple occasions being told "oh you can just try again". NO! I wanted that baby. I wanted Taylor just like I wanted Amaiya and Ava. One child can never replace another. The hardest part of losing a child is the fear of trying again. Through my experience I have learned that we cannot control fate. Fear will hold you back from enjoying the blessings you have and the blessings you have to come. It wasn't until I put my hurt and pain in the hands of God, that I began to accept what happened, grieve, and grow from it. There's a time and a season for everything and it was my time to speak out. I have not stopped telling my story and I do not intend to ever stop. If you ask me how many children I have, I will always say three and I will not explain who's living and who's not. I have three beautiful daughters and I love them all equally. But I still mourn and cry for Taylor. I have moments where I cry hard for long periods of time. It's okay to cry. I miss her very much and it still hurts as if it just happened. The difference is I now know how to deal with my loss and not be stuck. We're going to mourn forever.

The worse times in my life created what is now the best version of me. Every individual person feels emotions differently and will grieve at their own pace. It can't be forced, and it can't be suppressed, or it'll make matters worse, trust me I know. The average person does not know what it is like to bury their child, therefore the way they perceive you and your actions are going to come off insensitive, mostly from lack of understanding. What I learned and try to instill in others is that we cannot control how others feel, we can only control what we feel. Let's not make life harder by reacting to the insensitivity in a negative way. Let's rise above and teach people what they may not know. I took my experience of loss and turned it into a gain for myself and for those that rely on me. Starting We Heard You was the best thing I could have ever done. It's been my own personal therapy. Helping others, especially children is the best satisfaction for me. I would not do it differently because of the many lives I have been able to positively impact. If I reach just one person, I've done my part. I took that hurt and pain and turned it into something positive.

Keep going. I believe in you.

What am I doing now?

I'm in love

I can honestly say that there was a substantial time in my life where I had completely given up on love. I did not want to try to love anyone. I did not want anyone to be in love with me. I just wanted to be in my own space and be happy. It feels so great and refreshing to say that I tried again and I'm in love; we're in love. To have a man pray for you and with you is invaluable. Things aren't perfect, but nothing is, but we're happy and we're blessed. This feeling did not happen overnight. I am cherishing and savoring every single moment. I have a beautiful family. I have two healthy daughters and we have our angel watching over us forever. Trust me when I say this, if you're feeling hopeless and defeated, there is a light at the end of the tunnel. You have to dig deep to get there because nothing comes to you. It is ok to be still for a moment, but you have to remember to keep moving. If you've experienced any of the relationship heartache that I have, trust me when I say, **you will love again.** *Never stop trying.*

Unbelievable Bliss

The way that he loves me is dreamlike

Has me visualizing what being his wife would be like

Mrs. Paul, I slipped, but he caught my fall

Bearing his children is in my plan

Just a year ago this idea never stood a chance.

You can feel my heart when he speaks so full of passion; I'm ready.

Little by little he changes my way of thinking; I'm sinking.

Deeper and deeper, he makes me weaker, but in a good way

Even when I'm down he always brightens up my day

The vibe, I can't deny the butterflies; he's such a great guy!

He's so meek when he speaks, and he gently kisses my cheek

He holds me close and embraces me flaws and all

The thought of getting it right, no tears, no fights

My prayer for God to repair the despair that we both once shared

The past, the pain still remains sometimes I feel so ashamed

Thoughts about not wanting to lose him, use him, or confuse him

No holding back, it's meant to be

It's time we begin to write our own history

It's no mystery that the connection we share, no one can compare

A fresh start for my fragile heart

Who would've thought?

Our souls were entwined in such a short time

He gives me a piece of mind

To love and be loved in return, I've yearned.

I've waited patiently, GOD thank you for giving me my turn.

The pain has turned into laughter and love

This type of peace can only be given from above.

When he looks at me his eyes tell me I'm all that he needs

In a room, full of beautiful women his eyes tell me I'm all he sees

He's always in my prayers

I think God showed him my soul; I've been waiting

I'm convinced he's the one

By Cherese Akers

I'm Coping.

My life is far from perfect but coming from where I was to where I am now, I'm a living testament that through trials will come tribulations. I'm still in therapy. I only speak to my therapist once a month right now and that's just to touch base and to see how I've been coping. I thank God for therapy. I highly recommend keeping therapy consistent in your life after tragedy. It's a safe, unbiased space where you can express your true feelings or concerns without judgment. It's a professional support system that provides a great service. Be honest with yourself so that you can be honest with your therapist, it goes a long way. I have faith in you.

Scars let us know that although pain may have once lived in that space, it will heal. Scars show us that we can survive. Scars tell us that all wounds and incisions will be closed once again. So, cope because there is so much hope!

I'm Living. I'm alive.

I'm no longer living in fear, doubt, anger, resentment, etc. We only get one chance at this beautiful thing called life that God has given us. I felt dead, afraid, and incapable for so long. I refuse to allow life to keep putting me in the dumps over and over and I just stay there. I reclaimed my life and took back my power. I'm spreading love, advocacy, support, compassion, and positive vibes to all who will receive it. In life we make good and bad choices. Instead of dwelling on my bad choices, I'm focusing on the comeback. "IT'S ALL ABOUT THE COMEBACK", as my older sister would say. I'm taking accountability for my repeated offensives.

I dare you to live

Grow and forgive

Give thanks up above

Be free and fall in love

It's ok to shed tears

Just as long as you're aware

Be alive because you survived

I'm advocating.

I'm advocating for you and for myself. I'm advocating for the youth I serve and our communities. I'm advocating to bring awareness to pregnancy and infant loss. There is so much to be taught, so much to learn, so much to give. Through my new foundation, Still I Birthed, I will continue to share my experience and be a resource to anyone in need. I can't express how important it is that we share our experiences in order for healing and to possibly help heal someone else. I'm happy to report that more and more conversations and stories are surfacing. We're bringing awareness to pregnancy and infant loss one person at a time.

I stand with you. I am 1 in 4.

Stillbirth But I Still Birthed

What can be worse?

Carelessness from my nurse.

I buried my first.

Stillborn. My heart is torn. Let me mourn.

Family wondering what to say, go away, don't want to pray.

Just a shell. What the hell? I want to yell.

Block it out, what they talking 'bout.

What to do, no one knew, how to breakthrough, we can't undo,

what's the use.

A year later.

8th & Spruce. Labor induced. Stressed reduced.

Healthy baby number two.

Seven pounds, beautiful heartbeat sounds, I breakdown.

Don't surround. Don't come around. Shutdown.

Don't touch, made a fuss. Full of mistrust. I won't discuss.

How I'm feeling. The pain I'm concealing. I'm not healing.

The anger is revealing. Cut my dealings. Suicide sounds so

appealing.

Attack is my defense. Careless and fearless. Tearless. Won't let

anyone close enough. So heartless.

Summer of 2016. So carefree. All I ever needed was me.

God always shows you what you don't want to see.

The breakup was the best wakeup. The changeup. The glow up. The

grow up.

Stillbirth but I still birthed!

So brave. I forgave. Un-enslaved. I broke the chain.

Cannot explain. I'm not ashamed.

God I proclaim.

It's only you. Who could pull me through.

THANK YOU

I pushed through!

By Cherese Akers

October 15th

Wherever you are

Look up to the sky

Remember the babies

That had to say goodbye

A moment of silence

Light a candle

Say a prayer

Sing a song

On October 15th

Let your love ones know

You'll support them lifelong!

By Cherese Akers

A constant note and reminder to myself; You Got This!

A special thanks to:

My mom, Patricia, for being my rock! I know you'll always have my front and my back. I look to you for everything. You've been a praying and loving mother for as long as I can remember. I thank you for never giving up on me and never allowing anyone else to. You are the true definition of what I always wanted to be in a mother. I Love you!

Caneshia Bailey, Sheree Akers, Jasmine Johnson, Sherrell Brown, and Hermina Lezama for helping with making edits to the book and fleshing out content. To my sisters, *NeNe, Rell, Ree Ree, Jazz, and Bran* I love you guys so much. I appreciate all the support and love you give me. Thank you for encouraging me and always loving on me!

Constance Dogan for editing the entire book and for her contributions to the content of the book. Thank you for all of your support and love!

Nicole Doss for taking the time to help me self-publish and support me in the process from the beginning to the end. If it weren't for you, the deadline would've been further than it already was.

Shanell Vicks, Nina Murphy, Kiana Pace, Ashley McDonald, Danielle Collins, Liz Frisby, DaiNa Glean and *Carla Robinson:* To my amazing friends who have never left my side throughout this process and has supported all of my endeavors! Who loves all of my kids as if they were yours. I truly appreciate and love you all dearly!

Tiffany Frazier for giving me that PUSH I truly needed. As I always say, if it wasn't for HerStory, I would have never shared my story! Thank you for always encouraging me and supporting me!
Love you sis!

Anthony Hairston, I think I drove you crazy the most. You've always been the best big brother to me. I've always looked up to you and respected you. Thank you for always having my back and holding me down! You are a great man. Love you twin!

To the love of my life, *Val Paul*, words can't express what you mean to me. I thank God that he put us together. You've been such a blessing to me. Thank you for loving me and my babies the way you do. Thank you for being so patient with me. Thank you for your consistency. Thank you for everything! I love you!

References:

Opioid https://www.verywellhealth.com/opioid-induced-constipation-4153814

Made in the USA
Middletown, DE
29 September 2019